JAPAN

Ali Brownlie

Photographs by Masanori Kobayashi

CHERRYTREE BOOKS

Titles in this series

BANGLADESH • BRAZIL • CHINA • FRANCE • INDIA • ITALY • JAMAICA • JAPAN • KENYA • SPAIN

A Cherrytree Book

Conceived and produced by

Nutshell
MEDIA

Intergen House
65-67 Western Road
Hove BN3 2JQ, UK
www.nutshellmedialtd.co.uk

First published in 2003 by
Evans Brothers Ltd
2A Portman Mansions
Chiltern Street
London W1U 6NR

© Copyright Evans Brothers 2003

Editor: Katie Orchard
Designer: Tim Mayer
Map artwork: Encompass Graphics Ltd
All other artwork: Tim Mayer
Geography consultant: Jeff Stanfield, Geography
   Inspector for Ofsted
Literacy consultant: Anne Spiring

All photographs were taken by Masanori Kobayashi.

Printed in Hong Kong.

Acknowledgements
The author and photographer would like to thank the
following for their help: the Kobayashi family and the
teachers and pupils at Fumi's school in Osaka.

British Library Cataloguing in Publication Data
      Brownlie, Alison, 1949–
      Japan – (Letters From Around the World)
      1. Japan – Social conditions – 1945 – Juvenile
      literature
      2. Japan – Social life and customs – 1945 –
      Juvenile literature
      I. Title
      952'.05

ISBN 1 8423 4171 5

Cover: Fumi and his friends from baseball club.
Title page: Fumi takes aim in a baseball match.
This page: Mount Fuji – Japan's highest mountain.
Contents page: Fumi and his brother Sota ski in the
   mountains in Nagano.
Glossary: Fumi washes the windows from the balcony.
Further information page: Fumi's friend practises
   writing Japanese characters on the chalkboard.
Index: The tension mounts in a game of baseball.

Contents

My Country

Saturday, 5 January

7-1-14-564
Kitamidorigaoka
Osaka 560-0001
Japan

Dear Nicky,

Ossu! (This is how we say 'hi' in Japanese.)

My name is Fumi Kobayashi and I'm 9 years old. I live with my family in Osaka, a big city in Japan. I have a brother, Sota, who's 11, and a sister, Maya, who's 14. I'm really excited about being your pen-pal. I hope we can learn a lot about each other.

Write back soon!

From
Fumi

Here I am (in the middle) standing on a wall outside a Buddhist temple with Mum, Dad, Sota and Maya. →

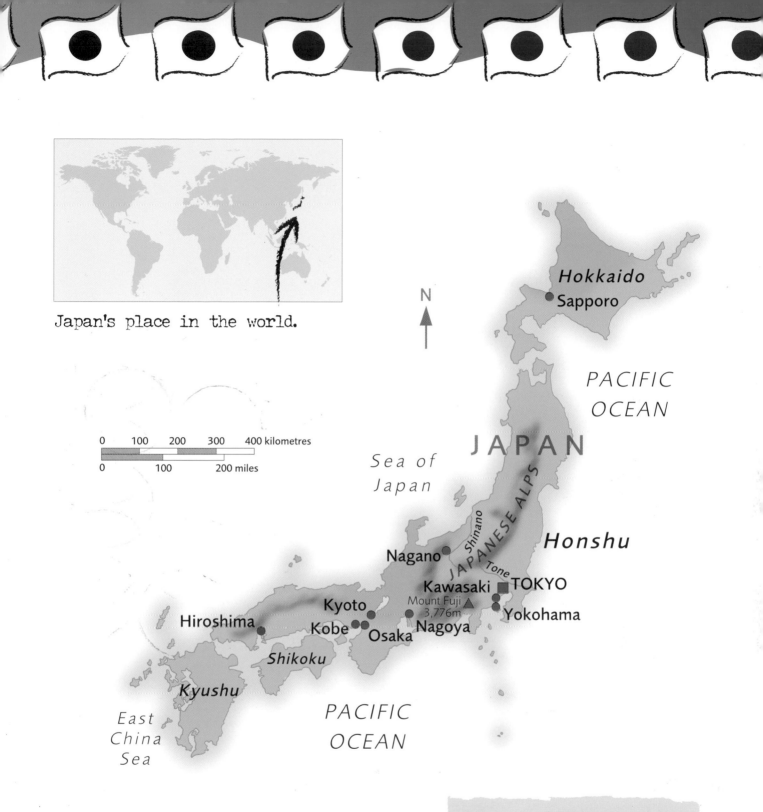

Japan's place in the world.

Sea of
Japan

Hokkaido
Sapporo

PACIFIC
OCEAN

JAPAN

Honshu

JAPANESE ALPS

Shinano

Nagano

Tone

Kawasaki
Mount Fuji
3,776m

TOKYO

Kyoto
Kobe
Osaka

Nagoya

Yokohama

Hiroshima

Shikoku

Kyushu

East
China
Sea

PACIFIC
OCEAN

Japan is made up of a chain of nearly 4,000 islands. Most people live on the four big islands of Honshu, Hokkaido, Shikoku and Kyushu.

This map shows the four main islands of Japan. Osaka is on Honshu.

Osaka is Japan's third-largest city. It has a population of 2.5 million. Osaka is over a thousand years old, but today it is a busy modern city with towering office blocks.

This is Midosuji, the main road of Osaka, which connects the north to the south.

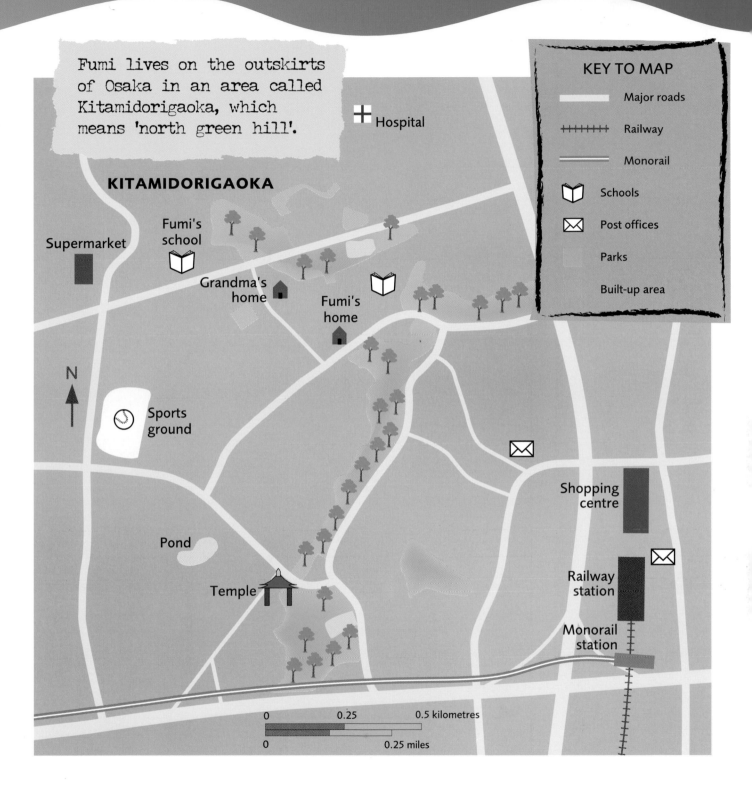

Fumi lives on the outskirts of Osaka in an area called Kitamidorigaoka, which means 'north green hill'.

Hospital

KEY TO MAP

Major roads
Railway
Monorail
Schools
Post offices
Parks
Built-up area

KITAMIDORIGAOKA

Supermarket

Fumi's school

Grandma's home

Fumi's home

N

Sports ground

Pond

Temple

Shopping centre

Railway station

Monorail station

0   0.25   0.5 kilometres

0   0.25 miles

Osaka is an important port. It is in the centre of Japan and is easy to reach by train, road, aeroplane or ship. Electronic goods are made in Osaka and leave the country by ship.

Landscape and Weather

Japan is very mountainous. The country has many volcanoes and earthquakes are common. Most towns and cities are in the narrow, flat coastal areas. Osaka is known as the 'city of water' because it has many rivers and is on the edge of a bay.

In the winter Fumi goes skiing in the mountains in Nagano, 450km north-east of Osaka.

Most of Japan has a mild, humid climate. But because it stretches so far from north to south, it can be hot in the south and freezing in the north.

Fumi picks oranges in his uncle's orchard in southern Kyushu. Oranges grow well in the warm climate there.

Osaka's Climate

January	July
Temperature	Temperature
6°C	28°C
113mm	139mm
Rainfall	Rainfall

At Home

In Japan there is very little flat land on which to build houses. Like most Japanese people, Fumi's family lives in a small flat in an apartment block. The flat has a balcony, where the family hangs out the washing.

Fumi and Sota stand together outside their apartment block.

One of Fumi's chores is to wash the windows on the balcony.

In a small flat it is important to keep everything tidy. Fumi does a lot of chores around the house. Sometimes he does the vacuuming and hangs out the washing. He also helps his mum with the shopping and cooking.

Space has to be used carefully in a small flat. The washing machine and dryer are stacked up in the bathroom.

Fumi's house has the very latest technology. His family owns two televisions, two computers, a dishwasher, a microwave and several stereos.

Fumi loves playing video games with his friends.

Fumi has his own bedroom. He does his homework at his desk just before he goes to bed.

Sunday, 10 March

7-1-14-564
Kitamidorigaoka
Osaka 560-0001
Japan

Hi Nicky!

Have I told you about our special room? Although we have lots of modern things, we keep one room in the old Japanese style. There is no furniture and we sit on cushions. The floor is covered with straw mats called *tatami*. We always take off our shoes or slippers before we go into this room.

What's your home like?

From
Fumi

When friends stay over, we sleep in our traditional room on mattresses on the floor called *futons*.

Food and Mealtimes

Fumi helps his mum carry the shopping back from the supermarket.

Fumi gets up at 7.30 a.m. For breakfast he usually has egg and toast, fruit, vegetable juice and a cup of tea. On schooldays he has his lunch at school. At home, lunch and dinner usually include rice or noodles.

Fumi eats lunch in his classroom with his friends.

Fumi's mum buys all the family's food at the supermarket. Fumi's family likes lots of different kinds of food, which they usually eat with chopsticks. Fumi's favourite foods are *sushi*, curry, and Western and Japanese-style pizza!

Fumi's family has a traditional Japanese meal of *sashimi*, which is raw fish.

Rice balls (*onigiri*) are usually eaten cold and are perfect for picnics.

Traditional Japanese food is very healthy. It is based on rice, fish and vegetables. *Sushi* is very popular. *Sushi* is made from sticky rice topped with, or wrapped round different kinds of fish or omelette.

Fumi's family enjoys eating out together. This is a fast-food tent at a festival.

Friday, 29 May

7-1-14-564
Kitamidorigaoka
Osaka 560-0001
Japan

Ossu Nicky!

Here's that *sushi* recipe you asked for.

You will need: 1 cup of short-grained rice, 1 cup water, 4 tablespoons rice vinegar, 1 tablespoon sugar, a small packet of smoked salmon, strips of cucumber, sheets of dried seaweed (you can buy this from a Japanese food shop).

1. Boil the rice in a saucepan until the water has gone.
2. Mix in the vinegar and sugar and leave to cool down.
3. Spread 2 tablespoons of rice on a sheet of dried seaweed.
4. Put a thin strip of salmon and cucumber on top and roll the seaweed round the filling to make an oblong.
5. Moisten the edge of the seaweed to make it stick, and slice into bite-sized pieces.

Try it dipped in soya sauce – it's delicious!

From
Fumi

Here I am rolling the *sushi* into an oblong.

17

School Day

Fumi goes to the primary school near his home.
Children at Fumi's school do not wear uniforms,
but they do have to wear the same sports kit.

Fumi usually walks to
school with his friends.

School starts at 8.25 a.m. and finishes at 3.30 p.m. Fumi's favourite subjects are sport and science. He also studies Japanese, maths, music, crafts, cooking and sewing.

The head teacher leads morning assembly in the school playground.

This is Fumi's classroom. There are 35 children in his class.

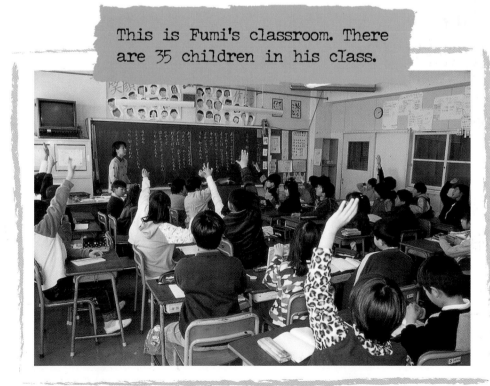

Fumi's mum has been teaching him English since he was 6 years old. He will have English lessons at school when he is 12.

Fumi's friend practises
writing Japanese characters
on the chalkboard.

Japanese writing is made
up of little pictures, called
characters. There are over
7,000 of them. Fumi has to
learn over 1,000 characters
at primary school.

Children serving lunch
wear masks so that
they do not breathe
germs on the food.

Fumi and his classmates
have to clean their own
classrooms, the toilets and
the playground. Everyone
takes it in turns to serve
school lunch.

Friday, 25 September

7-1-14-564
Kitamidorigaoka
Osaka 560-0001
Japan

Dear Nicky,

I'm glad you did well on your Japan project. Today was my favourite day of the year – school sports day. Some of my friends put on a gymnastics display and some ran races. I took part in the tug of war – it was great fun!

We love sport in Japan. On the second Monday of October we have a national sports day – it's a public holiday. What's your favourite sport?

From

Fumi

Here's my team
in the tug of war.
We won the
competition!

Off to Work

Fumi's mum is a high school teacher. She works part-time so she can look after the children when they come home from school. Fumi's dad is a photographer. His work takes him all over the world.

Fumi's mum sometimes gives extra lessons at her home to older students studying for exams.

In Japan, many people travel long distances by train every day to get to work.

These people are making electronic ticket barriers for Japan's train stations.

In Japan, many people work in shops and offices, or in the electronics industry. In Osaka there are lots of jobs in factories making cars and electronic equipment such as hi-fis and televisions.

Free Time

Fumi's dad is often away from home, so the family likes doing things together when they can. In the summer holidays they go swimming, fishing and camping together. In the winter they like skiing.

Fumi playing *shogi* with his friend. This is a Japanese version of chess.

Fumi's sister helps him practise the piano.

Fumi has baseball practice on Saturdays and matches almost every Sunday.

The Japanese love sport. Traditional sports such as judo and *sumo* wrestling are still popular, and many people are interested in football, baseball and basketball.

Religion and Festivals

Buddhists wash their hands before they enter a temple. They use special cups outside.

Like many Japanese people, Fumi and his family are Buddhists. Shinto is the other main religion in Japan.

In November there is a special festival called *Shichigosan*. This is when parents give thanks to the gods for the health of their children. Some children wear kimonos (traditional Japanese clothes).

Shichigosan means the ages of the children taking part — seven (*shichi*), five (*go*) and three (*san*).

Friday, 4 November

7-1-14-564
Kitamidorigaoka
Osaka 560-0001
Japan

Dear Nicky,

You wanted to know if we have any special festivals. We have lots! One special festival is *Obon* week, which is usually in July or August. We believe that the spirits of our ancestors visit us during this time. We visit our ancestors' graves and hang lanterns there. There are also special ceremonies at the temple. Then we float the lanterns on the river to guide the spirits home. It is really beautiful!

Sayonara
(This means goodbye.)

Fumi

During *Obon*, we had a special meal for my grandfather at the Buddhist temple.

Fact File

Capital city: The capital of Japan is Tokyo. It has a population of 8 million.

Other major cities: Yokohama, Osaka, Nagoya, Sapporo, Kobe and Kyoto.

Size: 378,000 km².

Population: 126.5 million.

Language: Japanese.

Flag: The Japanese flag is known as the *Hinomaru*. The red circle is the rising sun. Japan is sometimes called the 'Land of the Rising Sun'.

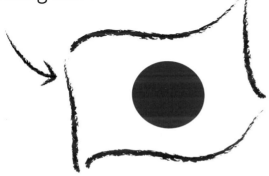

Main religions: Most people in Japan follow Buddhism or Shinto.

Currency: The Japanese currency is known as the yen.

Highest mountain: Mount Fuji (3,776m). Mount Fuji is a volcano. It last erupted in 1707.

Longest river: The longest river is the Shinano (367km).

Main industries: Japan exports cars, computers and electronic equipment all over the world.

Earthquakes: Japan has about 1,000 small earthquakes each year. Sometimes there is a major one. The last major earthquake happened in Kobe, in 1995. All Japanese children learn what to do if there is an earthquake while they are at school. They must get under their desks and hold on to the legs of the desk until the earthquake has stopped.

Volcanoes: Japan has 83 active volcanoes, some of which may have several eruptions every year.

Royal family: Japan's royal family can trace its ancestors back over 2,500 years. The current emperor, Emperor Akihito, calls his reign '*Heisei*', which means 'the achievement of complete peace'. The chrysanthemum is the symbol of the royal family.

Stamps: Japanese stamps show important buildings, art, birds and animals of Japan. Some celebrate historical events.

Bullet trains: The bullet train, or *shinkansen*, is one of the fastest trains in the world. It has a top speed of 300 kilometres per hour.

Glossary

ancestors Family members that have died.

balcony A platform outside a window, usually with railings.

earthquake A violent shaking of the Earth's surface. Earthquakes can cause a lot of damage.

futon A traditional Japanese bed, made from a cotton mattress on a wooden frame. It is rolled out at night and put away in the morning.

humid climate A warm and damp weather system.

judo A Japanese sport that is similar to wrestling.

Obon **week** A special festival during which Japanese people remember their ancestors.

port A place where ships can load and unload their cargoes.

sashimi A traditional Japanese meal made from small pieces of raw fish.

sumo **wrestling** One of the most popular Japanese sports. The wrestlers are very heavy and try to topple each other outside the wrestling circle.

sushi A Japanese dish made from flavoured sticky rice wrapped around fish or omelette. *Sushi* can be made into balls or rolls.

tatami Thick straw mats that cover the floors of traditional Japanese rooms.

temple A place of worship.

Further Information

Information books:

Continents: Asia by Leila Merrell Foster (Heinemann, 2002)

The Changing Face of Japan (Hodder Wayland, 2002)

Fiesta!: Japan by Susie Dawson (Franklin Watts, 2001)

Food and Festivals: A Flavour of Japan by Teresa Fisher (Hodder Wayland, 1999)

Look What Came from Japan by Miles Harvey (Franklin Watts, 1999)

Make It Work! Japan by Andrew Haslam and Clare Doran (Two-Can Publishing, 2001)

We Come from Japan by Teresa Fisher (Hodder Wayland, 2002)

Fiction:

Grandfather Cherry-Blossom by Eiho Hirezaki; translated by Ralph F. McCarthy (Kodansha International, 2000)

Turtle Bay by Saviour Pirotta (Frances Lincoln, 1998)

Websites:

CIA World Factbook
www.cia.gov/cia/publications/factbook/
Facts and figures about Japan and other countries.

Japan Information Network
http://jin.jcic.or.jp/atlas/
A look at Japan's architecture, festivals and nature by region.

Kidsweb Japan
www.jinjapan.org/kidsweb/
This website has lots of basic facts and figures about Japan.

Index